THE ART OF WAR

SUN TZU

THE ART OF WAR

Translated by
THOMAS CLEARY

SHAMBHALA
Boston & London
1991

Shambhala Publications, Inc.
Horticultural Hall
300 Massachusetts Avenue
Boston, Massachusetts 02115

12   11   10

Printed in Hong Kong
⊗ This edition is printed on acid-free paper that
meets the American National
Standards Institute Z39.48 Standard.

Distributed in the United States by Random House, Inc.,
and in Canada by Random House of Canada Ltd

Cover art: Ceremonial ax (detail), Chinese bronze,
Shang period. Museum für Ostasiatische Kunst,
Staatliche Museen Preussicher Kulturbesitz, Berlin.

Library of Congress Cataloging-in-Publication Data
Sun-tzu, 6th cent. B.C.
[Sun-tzu ping fa. English]
The Art of war/Sun Tzu; translated by Thomas Cleary.
p.   cm.—(Shambhala pocket classics)
Translation of: Sun-tzu ping fa.
"An abridgment of the Shambhala Dragon edition of the
same title"—Pref.
ISBN 0-87773-537-9 (pbk.: acid-free paper)
1. Military art and science—Early works to 1800.   I. Cleary,
Thomas, 1949- .   II. Title.   III. Series.
U101.S95   1993c   90-52805
355'.02—dc20   CIP

CONTENTS

TRANSLATOR'S PREFACE

The Art of War, compiled well over two thousand years ago by a mysterious Chinese warrior-philosopher, is still perhaps the most prestigious and influential book of strategy in the world today, as eagerly studied in Asia by modern politicians and executives as it has been by military leaders and strategists for the last two millennia and more.

In Japan, which was transformed directly from a feudal culture into a corporate culture virtually overnight, contemporary students of *The Art of War* have applied the strategy of this ancient classic to modern politics and business with similar alacrity. Indeed, some see in the successes of postwar Japan an illustration of

Sun Tzu's dictum of the classic, "To win without fighting is best."

As a study of the anatomy of organizations in conflict, *The Art of War* applies to competition and conflict in general, on every level from the interpersonal to the international. Its aim is invincibility, victory without battle, and unassailable strength through understanding of the physics, politics, and psychology of conflict.

This translation of *The Art of War* presents the classic from the point of view of its background in the great spiritual tradition of Taoism. What is perhaps most characteristically Taoist about *The Art of War* in such a way as to recommend itself to the modern day is the manner in which power is continually tempered by a profound undercurrent of humanism. *The Art of War* is thus a book not only of war but also of peace, above all a tool for understanding the very roots of conflict and resolution.

EDITOR'S NOTE

This Shambhala Pocket Classics edition of *The Art of War* is an abridgment of the Shambhala Dragon Edition of the same title. It contains the complete text of Sun Tzu, in bold face, and selected commentaries.

TRANSLATOR'S INTRODUCTION

According to an old story, a lord of ancient China once asked his physician, a member of a family of healers, which of them was the most skilled in the art.

The physician, whose reputation was such that his name became synonymous with medical science in China, replied, "My eldest brother sees the spirit of sickness and removes it before it takes shape, so his name does not get out of the house.

"My elder brother cures sickness when it is still extremely minute, so his name does not get out of the neighborhood.

"As for me, I puncture veins, prescribe potions, and massage skin, so from time to time my name gets out and is heard among the lords."

Among the tales of ancient China, none

captures more beautifully than this the essence of *The Art of War,* the premier classic of the science of strategy in conflict. The healing arts and the martial arts may be a world apart in ordinary usage, but they are parallel in several senses: in recognizing, as the story says, that the less needed the better; in the sense that both involve strategy in dealing with disharmony; and in the sense that in both knowledge of the problem is key to the solution.

As in the story of the ancient healers, in Sun Tzu's philosophy the peak efficiency of knowledge and strategy is to make conflict altogether unnecessary. And like the story of the healers, Sun Tzu explains there are all grades of martial arts: The superior militarist foils enemies' plots; next best is to ruin their alliances; next after that is to attack their armed forces; worst is to besiege their cities.

This ideal strategy whereby one could win without fighting, accomplish the most by doing the least, bears the characteristic stamp of Taoism, the ancient tradition of knowledge that fostered both the healing arts and the martial arts in China. The ancient Taoist masters showed how the man of aggressive violence appears to be ruthless but is really an emotionalist; then they slay the emotionalist with real ruthlessness before revealing the spontaneous nature of free humanity.

Real ruthlessness, the coldness of complete objectivity, always includes oneself in its cutting assessment of the real situation. This is the ruthlessness of Lao-tzu when he says in the *Tao-te Ching* that the universe is inhumane and the sage sees people as being like the straw dogs used for ritual sacrifices. Chuang-tzu, another ancient Taoist master, also gives numerous dramatic illustrations of ruthlessness toward oneself as an exercise in perspective designed to lead to cessation of internal and external conflict.

This "inhumanity" is not used by the original philosophers as a justification for quasi-ruthless possessive aggression, but as a meditation on the ultimate meaninglessness of the greed and possessiveness that underlie aggression.

In India, Buddhist aspirants used to visit burning grounds and watch the corpses of those whose families couldn't afford a cremation rot away. This they did to terrify the greed and possessiveness out of themselves. After that they turned their minds toward thoughts of ideal individuals and ideal societies.

Similarly, Master Sun has his readers dwell on the ravages of war, from its incipient phases of treachery and alienation to its extreme forms of incendiary attack and siege, viewed as a sort of mass cannibalism of human and natural resources. With this device he gives the reader an enhanced feeling for the significance of individual and social virtues espoused by the humanitarian pacifists.

Paradox is often thought of as a standard device of Taoist psychology, used to cross imperceptible barriers of awareness. Perhaps the paradox of *The Art of War* is in its opposition to war. And as *The Art of War* wars against war, it does so by its own principles; it infiltrates the enemy's lines, uncovers the enemy's secrets, and changes the hearts of the enemy's troops.

The commentary in this translation has been selected from a standard collection of eleven interpreters who lived from the second to twelfth centuries C.E.

I
STRATEGIC
ASSESSMENTS

**Military action is important to the
nation—it is the ground of death
and life, the path of survival and
destruction, so it is imperative to
examine it.**

The ground means the location, the place
of pitched battle—gain the advantage and
you live, lose the advantage and you die.
Therefore military action is called the
ground of death and life. The path means
the way to adjust to the situation and establish victory—find this and you survive,
lose this and you perish.

**Therefore measure in terms of five
things, use these assessments to**

make comparisons, and thus find out what the conditions are. The five things are the way, the weather, the terrain, the leadership, and discipline.

These are to be assessed at headquarters — first assess yourself and your opponent in terms of these five things, deciding who is superior. Then you can determine who is likely to prevail.

The Way means inducing the people to have the same aim as the leadership, so that they will share death and share life, without fear of danger.

The Way means humaneness and justice. In ancient times a famous minister of state asked a political philosopher about military matters. The philosopher said, "Humaneness and justice are the means by which to govern properly. When government is carried out properly, people feel close to the leadership and think little of dying for it."

The weather means the seasons.

In ancient times many soldiers lost their fingers to frostbite on campaigns against the Huns, and many soldiers died of plague on campaigns against the southern tribes. This was because of carrying out operations in winter and summer.

The terrain is to be assessed in terms of distance, difficulty or ease of travel, dimension, and safety.

In any military operation, it is important first to know the lay of the land. When you know the distance to be traveled, then you can plan whether to proceed directly or by a circuitous route. When you know the difficulty or ease of travel, then you can determine the advantages of infantry or mounted troops. When you know the dimensions of the area, then you can assess how many troops you need, many or few. When you know the relative safety of the terrain, then you can discern whether to do battle or disperse.

Leadership is a matter of intelligence, trustworthiness, humaneness, courage, and sternness.

The Way of the ancient kings was to consider humaneness foremost, while the martial artists considered intelligence foremost. This is because intelligence involves ability to plan and to know when to change effectively. Trustworthiness means to make people sure of punishment or reward. Humaneness means love and compassion for people, being aware of their toils. Courage means to seize opportunities to make certain of victory, without vacillation. Sternness means to establish discipline in the ranks by strict punishments.

Discipline means organization, chain of command, and logistics.

Organization means that the troops must be grouped in a regulated manner. Chain of command means that there must be officers to keep the troops together and lead them. Logistics means overseeing supplies.

Every general has heard of these five things. Those who know them prevail, those who do not know them do not prevail.

Therefore use these assessments for comparison, to find out what the conditions are. That is to say, which political leadership has the Way? Which general has ability? Who has the better climate and terrain? Whose discipline is effective? Whose troops are the stronger? Whose officers and soldiers are the better trained? Whose system of rewards and punishments is clearer? This is how you can know who will win.

The ancient classic of documents says, "The one who treats me well is my leader, the one who treats me cruelly is my enemy." The question is, which side has a humane government, and which side has a cruel government.

> Assess the advantages in taking advice, then structure your forces accordingly, to supplement extraordinary tactics. Forces are to be structured strategically, based on what is advantageous.

> A military operation involves deception. Even though you are competent, appear to be incompetent. Though effective, appear to be ineffective.

This means that when you are really competent and effective you outwardly appear to be incompetent and ineffective, so as to cause the enemy to be unprepared.

Deception is for the purpose of seeking victory over an enemy; to command a group requires truthfulness.

When you are going to attack nearby, make it look as if you are going to go a long way; when you are going to attack far away, make it look as if you are going just a short distance.

Draw them in with the prospect of gain, take them by confusion.

When the states of Wu and Yue were at war with each other, Wu sent out three thousand criminals to give an appearance of disorder so as to lure Yue. Some of the criminals ran, some of them gave up; the Yue army fought with them, only to be defeated by the army of Wu.

When they are fulfilled, be prepared against them; when they are strong, avoid them.

If the enemy's government is fulfilled—meaning that there is mutual love between the rulers and the ruled, there is clarity and trustworthiness in the system of rewards and punishments, and the soldiers are well trained—then you should be on guard against them. Do not wait for a clash to make your preparations.

Use anger to throw them into disarray.

When their military leadership is obstreperous, you should irritate them to make them angry—then they will become impetuous and ignore their original strategy.

Use humility to make them haughty. Tire them by flight. Cause division among them. Attack when they are unprepared, make your move when they do not expect it.

Strike at their gaps, attack when they are lax, don't let the enemy figure out how to prepare. This is why it is said that in military operations formlessness is the most effective. One of the great warrior-leaders said, "The most efficient of movements is the one that is unexpected; the best of plans is the one that is unknown."

The formation and procedure used by the military should not be divulged beforehand.

To divulge means to leak out. The military has no constant form, just as water has no constant shape—adapt as you face the enemy, without letting them know beforehand what you are going to do. Therefore, assessment of the enemy is in the mind, observation of the situation is in the eyes.

The one who figures on victory at headquarters before even doing battle is the one who has the most strategic factors on his side. The one who figures on inability to prevail at headquarters before doing battle is the one who has the least strategic factors on his side. The one with many strategic fac-

tors in his favor wins, the one with few strategic factors in his favor loses—how much the more so for one with no strategic factors in his favor. Observing the matter in this way, I can see who will win and who will lose.

When your strategy is deep and far-reaching, then what you gain by your calculations is much, so you can win before you even fight. When your strategic thinking is shallow and near-sighted, then what you gain by your calculations is little, so you lose before you do battle. Therefore it is said that victorious warriors win first and then go to war, while defeated warriors go to war first and then seek to win.

2

DOING BATTLE

When you do battle, even if you are winning, if you continue for a long time it will dull your forces and blunt your edge; if you besiege a citadel, your strength will be exhausted. If you keep your armies out in the field for a long time, your supplies will be insufficient.

Arms are tools of ill omen—to employ them for an extended period of time will bring about calamity. As it is said, "Those who like to fight and so exhaust their military inevitably perish."

When your forces are dulled, your edge is blunted, your strength is exhausted, and your supplies are gone, then others will take advan-

tage of your debility and rise up. Then even if you have wise advisers you cannot make things turn out well in the end.

Therefore I have heard of military operations that were clumsy but swift, but I have never seen one that was skillful and lasted a long time. It is never beneficial to a nation to have a military operation continue for a long time.

As it is said, be swift as the thunder that peals before you have a chance to cover your ears, fast as the lightning that flashes before you can blink your eyes.

Therefore, those who are not thoroughly aware of the disadvantages in the use of arms cannot be thoroughly aware of the advantages in the use of arms.

Those who use the military skillfully do not raise troops twice and do not provide food three times.

This means you draft people into service once and then immediately seize victory — you do not go back to your country a second time to raise more troops. At first you provide food, after that you feed off the enemy.

By taking equipment from your own country but feeding off the enemy you can be sufficient in both arms and provisions.

When a country is impoverished by military operations, it is because of transporting supplies to a distant place. Transport supplies to a distant place, and the populace will be impoverished.

Those who are near the army sell at high prices. Because of high prices, the wealth of the common people is exhausted.

When supplies are transported far away, the people are worn out by the expense.

In the markets near the army, the prices of goods shoot up. Therefore long military campaigns are a plague to a nation.

> When resources are exhausted, then levies are made under pressure. When power and resources are exhausted, then the homeland is drained. The common people are deprived of seventy percent of their budget, while the government's expenses for equipment amount to sixty percent of its budget.

The people are the basis of a country, food is the heaven of the people. Those who rule over others should respect this and be sparing.

> Therefore a wise general strives to feed off the enemy. Each pound of food taken from the enemy is equivalent to twenty pounds you provide by yourself.

It takes twenty pounds of provisions to deliver one pound of provisions to a distant army.

So what kills the enemy is anger, what gets the enemy's goods is reward.

If you reward your men with spoils, that will make them fight on their own initiative, so the enemy's goods can be taken. That is why it is said that where there are big rewards there are valiant men.

Therefore, in a chariot battle, reward the first to capture at least ten chariots.

If you reward everyone, there will not be enough to go around, so you offer a reward to one in order to encourage everyone.

Change their colors, use them mixed in with your own. Treat the soldiers well, take care of them.

Captured soldiers should be well treated, to get them to work for you.

This is called overcoming the opponent and increasing your strength to boot.

If you use the enemy to defeat the enemy, you will be strong wherever you go.

So the important thing in a military operation is victory, not persistence.

Persistence is not profitable. An army is like fire—if you don't put it out, it will burn itself out.

Hence, we know that the leader of the army is in charge of the lives of the people and safety of the nation.

3

PLANNING
A SIEGE

The general rule for use of the military is that it is better to keep a nation intact than to destroy it. It is better to keep an army intact than to destroy it, better to keep a division intact than to destroy it, better to keep a battalion intact than to destroy it, better to keep a unit intact than to destroy it.

Wei Liaozi said, "Practicing martial arts, assess your opponents; cause them to lose spirit and direction so that even if the opposing army is intact it is useless—this is winning by the Tao. If you destroy the opposing army and kill the generals, mount the ramparts shooting, gather a mob and usurp the land, this is winning by force."

Therefore those who win every battle are not really skillful—those who render others' armies helpless without fighting are the best of all.

The superior militarist strikes while schemes are being laid. The next best is to attack alliances. The next best is to attack the army.

To be good at successful attack, deploying your forces without a hitch, is yet another notch down. Therefore a great warrior-emperor said, "One who fights for victory in front of bared blades is not a good general."

The lowest is to attack a city. Siege of a city is only done as a last resort.

Take three months to prepare your machines and three months to complete your siege engineering.

Some say that Master Sun's point here is that you shouldn't get angry and rush to attack. This is why he says to take time.

> If the general cannot overcome his anger and has his army swarm over the citadel, killing a third of his soldiers, and yet the citadel is still not taken, this is a disastrous attack.

> Therefore one who is good at martial arts overcomes others' forces without battle, conquers others' cities without siege, destroys others' nations without taking a long time.

A skillful martialist ruins plans, spoils relations, cuts off supplies, or blocks the way, and hence can overcome people without fighting.

> It is imperative to contest all factions for complete victory, so the army is not garrisoned and the

profit can be total. This is the law of strategic siege.

Complete victory is when the army does not fight, the city is not besieged, the destruction does not go on long, but in each case the enemy is overcome by strategy.

So the rule for use of the military is that if you outnumber the opponent ten to one, then surround them; five to one, attack; two to one, divide.

If you are equal, then fight if you are able. If you are fewer, then keep away if you are able. If you are not as good, then flee if you are able.

This advice applies to the case where all else is equal. If your forces are orderly while theirs are chaotic, if you are excited and they are sluggish, then even if they are more numerous you can do battle. If your soldiers, strength, strategy, and courage are all less than that of the opponent, then you should retreat and watch for an opening.

> **Therefore if the smaller side is stubborn, it becomes the captive of the larger side.**

This means that if a small country does not assess its power and dares to become the enemy of a large country, no matter how firm its defenses be, it will inevitably become a captive nation. The *Spring and Autumn Annals* say, "If you cannot be strong, and yet cannot be weak, this will result in your defeat."

> **Generals are assistants of the nation. When their assistance is complete, the country is strong. When their assistance is defective, the country is weak.**

If the generals do not help the leadership, and harbor duplicity in their hearts, then the country will be weak. Therefore it is imperative to be careful in choosing people for positions of responsibility.

So there are three ways in which a civil leadership causes the military trouble. When a civil leadership unaware of the facts tells its armies to advance when it should not, or tells its armies to retreat when it should not, this is called tying up the armies. When the civil leadership is ignorant of military affairs but shares equally in the government of the armies, the soldiers get confused. When the civil leadership is ignorant of military maneuvers but shares equally in the command of the armies, the soldiers hesitate. Once the armies are confused and hesitant, trouble comes from competitors. This is called taking away victory by deranging the military.

If you try to use the methods of civilian government to govern a military operation, the operation will become confused.

> So there are five ways of knowing who will win. Those who know when to fight and when not to fight are victorious. Those who discern when to use many or few troops are victorious. Those whose upper and lower ranks have the same desire are victorious. Those who face the unprepared with preparation are victorious. Those whose generals are able and are not constrained by their governments are victorious. These five are the ways to know who will win.

To talk about government orders for all this is like going to announce to your superiors that you want to put out a fire — by the time you get back with an order, there is nothing left but ashes.

So it is said that if you know others and know yourself, you will not be imperiled in a hundred battles; if you do not know others but know yourself, you win one and lose one; if you do not know others and do not know yourself, you will be imperiled in every single battle.

4
FORMATION

In ancient times skillful warriors first made themselves invincible, and then watched for vulnerability in their opponents.

Making yourself invincible means knowing yourself; waiting for vulnerability in opponents means knowing others.

Invincibility is in oneself, vulnerability is in the opponent.

Therefore skillful warriors are able to be invincible, but they cannot cause opponents to be vulnerable.

If opponents have no formation to find out, no gap or slack to take advantage of, how can you overcome them even if you are well equipped?

That is why it is said that victory can be discerned but not manufactured.

Invincibility is a matter of defense, vulnerability is a matter of attack.

As long as you have not seen vulnerable formations in opponents, you hide your own form, preparing yourself in such a way as to be invincible, in order to preserve yourself. When opponents have vulnerable formations, then it is time to go out to attack them.

Defense is for times of insufficiency, attack is for times of surplus.

Those skilled in defense hide in the deepest depths of the earth, those skilled in attack maneuver in the highest heights of the sky. Therefore they can preserve themselves and achieve complete victory.

In defense, you hush your voices and obliterate your tracks, hidden as ghosts and spirits beneath and earth, invisible to anyone. On the attack, your movement is swift and your cry shattering, fast as thunder and lightning, as though coming from the sky, impossible to prepare for.

To perceive victory when it is known to all is not really skillful. Everyone calls victory in battle good, but it is not really good.

Everyone says victory in battle is good, but if you see the subtle and notice the hidden so as to seize victory where there is no form, this is really good.

It does not take much strength to lift a hair, it does not take sharp eyes to see the sun and moon, it does not take sharp ears to hear a thunderclap.

What everyone knows is not called wisdom, victory over others by forced battle is not considered good.

In ancient times those known as good warriors prevailed when it was easy to prevail.

If you are only able to ensure victory after engaging an opponent in armed conflict, that victory is a hard one. If you see the subtle and notice the hidden, breaking through before formation, that victory is an easy one.

Therefore the victories of good warriors are not noted for cleverness or bravery. Therefore their victories in battle are not flukes. Their victories are not flukes because they position themselves where they will surely win, prevailing over those who have already lost.

Great wisdom is not obvious, great merit is not advertised. When you see the subtle, it is easy to win — what has it to do with bravery or cleverness? When trouble is solved before it forms, who calls that clever? When there is victory without battle, who talks about bravery?

So it is that good warriors take their stand on ground where they cannot lose, and do not overlook conditions that make an opponent prone to defeat.

Therefore a victorious army first wins and then seeks battle; a defeated army first battles and then seeks victory.

This is the difference between those with strategy and those without forethought.

Those who use arms well cultivate the Way and keep the rules. Thus they can govern in such a way as to prevail over the corrupt.

Using harmony to hunt down opposition, not attacking a blameless country, not taking captives or booty wherever the army goes, not razing the trees or polluting the wells, washing off and purifying the shrines of the towns and hills in the countryside you pass through, not repeating the mistakes of a moribund nation—all this is called the Way and its rules. When the army is strictly disciplined, to the point where soldiers would die rather than disobey, rewards and punishments that are trustworthy and just are established—when the military leadership is such that it can achieve this, it can prevail over an opponent's corrupt civil government.

The rules of the military are five: measurement, assessment, calculation, comparison, and victory. The ground gives rise to measurements, measurements give rise to assessments, assessments give rise to calculations, calculations give rise to comparisons, comparisons give rise to victories.

By the comparisons of measurements you know where victory and defeat lie.

Therefore a victorious army is like a pound compared to a gram, a defeated army is like a gram compared to a pound.

When the victorious get their people to go to battle as if they were directing a massive flood of water into a deep canyon, this is a matter of formation.

When water accumulates in a deep canyon, no one can measure its amount, just as our defense shows no form. When the water is released it rushed down in a torrent, just as our attack is irresistible.

5
FORCE

Force means shifts in accumulated energy or momentum. Skillful warriors are able to allow the force of momentum to seize victory for them without exerting their strength.

> **Governing a large number as though governing a small number is a matter of division into groups. Battling a large number as though battling a small number is a matter of forms and calls.**

Forms and calls refer to the formations and signals used to dispose troops and co-ordinate movements.

> **Making the armies able to take on opponents without being defeated**

**is a matter of unorthodox and or-
thodox methods.**

Orthodoxy and unorthodoxy are not
fixed, but are like a cycle. Emperor Tai-
zong of the Tang dynasty, a famous warrior
and administrator, spoke of manipulating
opponents' perceptions of what is orthodox and what is unorthodox, then attacking unexpectedly, combining both into
one, becoming inscrutable to opponents.

**For the impact of armed forces to
be like stones thrown on eggs is a
matter of emptiness and fullness.**

When you induce opponents to come to
you, then their force is always empty; as
long as you do not go to them, your force
is always full. Attacking emptiness with
fullness is like throwing stones on eggs —
the eggs are sure to break.

**In battle, confrontation is done,
directly, victory is gained by surprise.**

Therefore those skilled at the unorthodox are infinite as heaven and earth, inexhaustible as the great rivers. When they come to an end, they begin again, like the days and months; they die and are reborn, like the four seasons.

Sun and moon travel through the sky, they set and rise again. The four seasons succeed one another, flourishing and then fading again. This is a metaphor for the interchange of surprise unorthodox movements and orthodox direct confrontation, mixing together into a whole, ending and beginning infinitely.

There are only five notes in the musical scale, but their variations are so many that they cannot all be heard. There are only five basic colors, but their variations are so many that they cannot all be seen. There are only five basic flavors, but their variations are so many that they cannot all be tasted. There are only two kinds of charge in battle, the unorthodox surprise attack and the orthodox direct attack, but variations of the unorthodox and the orthodox are endless. The unorthodox and the orthodox give rise to each other, like a beginningless circle—who could exhaust them?

When the speed of rushing water reaches the point where it can move boulders, this is the force of momentum. When the speed of a hawk is such that it can strike and kill, this is precision. So it is with skillful warriors—their force is swift, their precision is close. Their force is like drawing a catapult, their precision is like releasing the trigger.

Their force is swift in the sense that the force of the momentum of battle kills when it is released—that is why it is likened to a drawn catapult.

Disorder arises from order, cowardice arises from courage, weakness arises from strength.

What this means is that if you want to feign disorder so as to lead opponents on, first you must have complete order, for only then can you create artificial disorder. If you want to feign cowardice to spy on opponents, first you must be extremely brave, for only then can you act artificially timid. If you want to feign weakness to induce haughtiness in opponents, first you must be extremely strong, for only then can you pretend to be weak.

Order and disorder are a matter of organization, courage and cowardice are a matter of momentum, strength and weakness are a matter of formation.

When an army has the force of momentum, even the timid become brave; when it loses the force of momentum, even the brave become timid. Nothing is fixed in the laws of warfare—they develop based on momenta.

Therefore those who skillfully move opponents make formations that opponents are sure to follow, give what opponents are sure to take. They move opponents with the prospect of gain, waiting for them in ambush.

Formations that opponents are sure to follow are formations that give the impression of exhaustion. Opponents are moved by the prospect of an advantage.

Therefore good warriors seek effectiveness in battle from the force of momentum, not from individual people. Therefore they are able to choose people and let the force of momentum do its work.

When you have the force of momentum in war, even the timid can be courageous. So it is possible to choose them for their capabilities and give them the appropriate responsibilities. The brave can fight, the careful can guard, the intelligent can communicate. No one is useless.

Getting people to fight by letting the force of momentum work is like rolling logs and rocks. Logs and rocks are still when in a secure place, but roll on an incline; they remain stationary if square, they roll if round. Therefore, when people are skillfully led into battle, the momentum is like that of round rocks rolling down a high mountain—this is force.

6

EMPTINESS AND FULLNESS

Those who are first on the battle-field and await the opponents are at ease; those who are last on the battlefield and head into battle get worn out.

Therefore good warriors cause others to come to them, and do not go to others.

If you make opponents come to fight, then their force will always be empty. If you do not go to fight, then your force will always be full. This is the art of emptying others and filling yourself.

What causes opponents to come of their own accord is the prospect of gain. What discourages opponents from coming is the prospect of harm.

So when opponents are at ease, it is possible to tire them. When they are well fed, it is possible to starve them. When they are at rest, it is possible to move them.

You attack unexpectedly, causing opponents to become exhausted just running for their lives. You burn their supplies and raze their fields, cutting off their supply routes. You appear at critical places and strike when they least expect it, making them have to go to the rescue.

Appear where they cannot go, head for where they least expect you. To travel hundreds of miles without fatigue, go over land where there are no people.

Striking at an open gap does not only mean where the opponent has no defense.

As long as the defense is not strict, the place is not tightly guarded, they will fall apart in front of you, as if you were traveling over unpopulated territory.

> To unfailingly take what you attack, attack where there is no defense. For unfailingly secure defense, defend where there is no attack.

> So in the case of those who are skilled in attack, their opponents do not know where to defend. In the case of those skilled in defense, their opponents do not know where to attack.

When directives are carried out, people are sincerely loyal, preparations for defense are firmly secured, and yet you are so subtle and secretive that you reveal no form, opponents are unsure — their intelligence is of no avail.

> Be extremely subtle, even to the point of formlessness. Be ex-

tremely mysterious, even to the point of soundlessness. Thereby you can be the director of the opponent's fate.

To advance irresistibly, push through their gaps. To retreat elusively, outspeed them.

Military conditions are based on speed—come like the wind, go like lightning, and opponents will be unable to overcome you.

Therefore when you want to do battle, even if the opponent is deeply entrenched in a defensive position, he will be unable to avoid fighting if you attack where he will surely go to the rescue.

When you do not want to do battle, even if you draw a line on the ground to hold, the opponent cannot fight with you because you set him off on the wrong track.

This means that when opponents come to attack you, you do not fight with them but rather set up a strategic change to confuse them and make them uncertain.

Therefore when you induce others to construct a formation while you yourself are formless, then you are concentrated while the opponent is divided.

What is orthodox to you, make opponents see as unorthodox; what is unorthodox to you, make them see as orthodox. This is inducing others to construct a formation. Once the opponent's formation is seen, you then mass your troops against it. Since your form is not revealed, the opponent will surely divide up his forces for security.

When you are concentrated into one while the opponent is divided into ten, you are attacking at a concentration of ten to one, so you outnumber the opponent.

If you can strike few with many, you will thus minimize the num-

ber of those with whom you do battle.

While being deeply entrenched and highly barricaded, not allowing any information about yourself to become known, go out and in formlessly, attacking and taking unfathomably.

Your battleground is not to be known, for when it cannot be known, the enemy makes many guard outposts, and since multiple outposts are established, you only have to do battle with small squads.

So when the front is prepared, the rear is lacking, and when the rear is prepared the front is lacking. Preparedness on the left means lack on the right, preparedness on the right means lack on the left. Preparedness everywhere means lack everywhere.

This means that when troops are on guard in many places, they are perforce scattered into small bands.

The few are those on the defensive against others, the many are those who cause others to be on the defensive against themselves.

The more defenses you induce your enemy to adopt, the more impoverished your enemy will be.

So if you know the place and time of battle, you can join the fight from a thousand miles away. If you do not know the place and time of battle, then your left flank cannot save your right, your right cannot save your left, your vanguard cannot save your reaguard, and your reaguard cannot save your vanguard, even in a short range of a few to a few dozen miles.

According to my assessment, even if you have many more troops than

others, how can that help you to victory?

If you do not know the place and time of battle, even though your troops outnumber others, how can you know whether you will win or lose?

So it is said that victory can be made.

If you cause opponents to be unaware of the place and time of battle, you can always win.

Even if opponents are numerous, they can be made not to fight.

So assess them to find out their plans, both the successful ones and the failures. Incite them to action in order to find out the patterns of their movement and rest.

Do something for or against them, making opponents turn their attention to it, so that you can find out their patterns of aggressive and defensive behavior.

Induce them to adopt specific formations, in order to know the ground of death and life.

This means that you use many methods to confuse and disturb enemies to observe the forms of their response to you; after that you deal with them accordingly, so you can know what sort of situations mean life and what sort of situations mean death.

Test them to find out where they are sufficient and where they are lacking.

Therefore the consummation of forming an army is to arrive at formlessness. When you have no form, undercover espionage cannot find out anything, intelligence cannot form a strategy.

Once you have no perceptible form, you leave no traces to follow, so spies cannot find any chinks to see through and those in charge of intelligence cannot put any plans into operation.

Victory over multitudes by means of formation is unknowable to the multitudes. Everyone knows the form by which I am victorious, but no one knows the form by which I ensure victory.

Therefore victory in war is not repetitious, but adapts its form endlessly.

Determining changes as appropriate, do not repeat former strategies to gain victory. Whatever formations opponents may adopt, from the beginning I can adapt to them to attain victory.

Military formation is like water— the form of water is to avoid the high and go to the low, the form

of a military force is to avoid the full and attack the empty; the flow of water is determined by the earth, the victory of a military force is determined by the opponent.

So a military force has no constant formation, water has no constant shape: the ability to gain victory by changing and adapting according to the opponent is called genius.

7

ARMED
STRUGGLE

The ordinary rule for use of military force is for the military command to receive the orders from the civilian authorities, then to gather and mass the troops, quartering them together. Nothing is harder than armed struggle.

To fight with people face to face over advantages is the hardest thing in the world.

The difficulty of armed struggle is to make long distances near and make problems into advantages.

While giving the appearance of being far away, you step up your pace and get there before the opponent.

Therefore you make their route a long one, luring them on in hopes of gain. When you set out after others and arrive before them, you know the strategy of making the distant near.

You use a special squad to lure the opponent on a wild goose chase, making it seem as though your main force is far away; then you send out a surprise attack force that gets there first, even though it sets out last.

Therefore armed struggle is considered profitable, and armed struggle is considered dangerous.

For the skilled it is profitable, for the unskilled it is dangerous.

To mobilize the whole army to struggle for advantage would take too long, yet to struggle for advantage with a stripped-down army results in a lack of equipment.

So if you travel light, not stopping day or night, doubling your usual pace, struggling for an advantage a hundred miles away, your military leaders will be captured. Strong soldiers will get there first, the weary later on—as a rule, one in ten make it.

When the road is long the people are weary; if their strength has been used up in travel, then they are worn out while their opponents are fresh, so they are sure to be attacked.

Struggling for an advantage fifty miles away will thwart the forward leadership, and as a rule only fifty percent of the soldiers make it.

Struggle for an advantage thirty miles away, and two out of three get there.

So an army perishes if it has no equipment, it perishes if it has no food, and it perishes if it has no money.

These three things are necessary — you cannot fight to win with an unequipped army.

> So if you do not know the plans of your competitors, you cannot make informed alliances.

> Unless you know the mountains and forests, the defiles and impasses, and the lay of the marshes and swamps, you cannot maneuver with an armed force. Unless you use local guides, you cannot get the advantages of the land.

Only when you know every detail of the lay of the land can you maneuver and contend.

> So a military force is established by deception, mobilized by gain, and adapted by division and combination.

A military force is established by deception in the sense that you deceive enemies so that they do not know your real condition, and then can establish supremacy. It is mobilized by gain in the sense that it goes into action when it sees an advantage. Dividing and recombining is done to confuse opponents and observe how they react to you, so that then you can adapt in such a way as to seize victory.

Therefore when it moves swiftly it is like the wind, when it goes slowly it is like a forest; it is rapacious as fire, immovable as mountains.

It is swift as the wind in that it comes without a trace and withdraws like lightning. It is like a forest in that it is orderly. It is rapacious as fire across a plain, not leaving a single blade of grass. It is immovable as a mountain when it garrisons.

It is as hard to know as the dark; its movement is like pealing thunder.

To plunder a locality, divide up your troops. To expand your territory, divide the spoils.

The rule for military operations is to feed off the enemy as much as possible. However, in localities where people do not have very much, it is necessary to divide up the troops into smaller groups to take what they need here and there, for only then will there be enough.

As for dividing the spoils, this means it is necessary to divide up the troops to guard what has been gained, not letting enemies get it.

Act after having made assessments. The one who first knows the measures of far and near wins—this is the rule of armed struggle.

The first to move is the guest, the last to move is the host. The guest has it hard, the host has it easy. Far and near means travel—fatigue, hunger, and cold arise from travel.

An ancient book of military order says, "Words are not heard, so cymbals and drums are made. Owing to lack of visibility, banners and flags are made." Cymbals, drums, banners and flags are used to focus and unify people's ears and eyes. Once people are unified, the brave cannot proceed alone, the timid cannot retreat alone— this is the rule for employing a group.

To unify people's ears and eyes means to make people look and listen in concert so that they do not become confused and disorderly. Signals are used to indicate directions and prevent individuals from going off by themselves.

So in night battles, you use many fires and drums, in daytime battles

you use many banners and flags, so as to manipulate people's ears and eyes.

You use many signals to startle their perceptions and make them fear your awesome martial power.

So you should take away the energy of their armies, and take away the heart of their generals.

First you must be capable of firmness in your own heart—only then can you take away the heart of opposing generals. This is why tradition says that people of former times had the heart to take away hearts, and the ancient law of charioteers says that when the basic mind is firm, fresh energy is victorious.

So morning energy is keen, midday energy slumps, evening energy recedes—therefore those skilled in use of arms avoid the keen energy and strike the slumping and reced-

ing. These are those who master energy.

Any weakling in the world will fight in a minute if he gets excited, but when it comes to actually taking up arms and seeking to do battle, this is being possessed by energy—when this energy wanes they will stop, get frightened, and feel regret. The reason that armies look upon strong enemies the way they look at virgin girls is that their aggressiveness is being taken advantage of, as they are stirred up over something.

Using order to deal with the disorderly, using calm to deal with the clamorous, is mastering the heart.

Unless your heart is wide open and your mind is orderly, you cannot be expected to be able to adapt responsively without limit, dealing with events unerringly, facing great and unexpected difficulties without upset, calmly handling everything without confusion.

> Standing your ground awaiting those far away, awaiting the weary in comfort, awaiting the hungry with full stomachs, is mastering strength.

This is what is meant by getting others to come to you while avoiding being induced to go to others.

> Avoiding confrontation with orderly ranks and not attacking great formations is mastering adaptation.

> So the rule for military operations is not to face a high hill and not to oppose those with their backs to a hill.

This means that when opponents are on high ground you shouldn't attack upward, and when they are charging downward you shouldn't oppose them.

Do not follow a feigned retreat. Do not attack crack troops.

If opponents suddenly run away before their energy has faded, there are surely ambushes lying in wait to attack your forces, so you should carefully restrain your officers from pursuit.

Do not eat food for their soldiers.

If the enemy suddenly abandon their food supplies, they should be tested first before eating, lest they be poisoned.

Do not stop an army on its way home.

Under these circumstances, an opponent will fight to the death.

A surrounded army must be given a way out.

Show them a way to life so that they will not be in the mood to fight to the death, and then you can take advantage of this to strike them.

Do not press a desperate enemy.

An exhausted animal will still fight, as a matter of natural law.

These are rules of military operations.

8
ADAPTATIONS

The general rule for military operations is that the military leadership receives the order from the civilian leadership to gather armies.

Let there be no encampment on difficult terrain. Let diplomatic relations be established at borders. Do not stay in barren or isolated territory.

When on surrounded ground, plot. When on deadly ground, fight.

Being on surrounded ground means there is steep terrain on all sides, with you in the middle, so that the enemy can come and go freely but you have a hard time getting out and back.

There are routes not to be followed, armies not to be attacked, citadels not to be besieged, territory not to be fought over, orders of civilian governments not to be obeyed.

Therefore generals who know all possible adaptations to take advantage of the ground know how to use military forces. If generals do not know how to adapt advantageously, even if they know the lay of the land they cannot take advantage of it.

If they rule armies without knowing the arts of complete adaptivity, even if they know what there is to gain, they cannot get people to work for them.

If you can change with the momentum of forces, then the advantage does not change, so the only ones who get hurt are others. Therefore there is no constant structure. If you can fully comprehend this principle, you can get people to work.

Therefore the considerations of the intelligent always include both benefit and harm. As they consider benefit, their work can expand; as they consider harm, their troubles can be resolved.

Benefit and harm are interdependent, so the enlightened always consider them.

Therefore what restrains competitors is harm, what keeps competitors busy is work, what motivates competitors is profit.

Wear enemies out by keeping them busy and not letting them rest. But you have to have done your own work before you can do this. This work means developing a strong militia, a rich nation, a harmonious society, and an orderly way of life.

So the rule of military operations is not to count on opponents not

coming, but to rely on having ways
of dealing with them; not to count
on opponents not attacking, but to
rely on having what cannot be attacked.

If you can always remember danger when
you are secure and remember chaos in
times of order, watch out for danger and
chaos while they are still formless and prevent them before they happen, this is best
of all.

Therefore, there are five traits that
are dangerous in generals. Those
who are ready to die can be killed;
those who are intent on living can
be captured; those who are quick
to anger can be shamed; those who
are puritanical can be disgraced;
those who love people can be trou-
bled.

If you appear in a place they are sure to
rush to defend, those who love the people

there will invariably hasten there to rescue them, troubling and wearying themselves in the process.

These five things are faults in generals, disasters for military operations.

Good generals are otherwise: they are not committed to death yet do not expect to live; they act in accord with events, not quick to anger, not subject to embarrassment. When they see possibility, they are like tigers, otherwise they shut their doors. Their action and inaction are matters of strategy, and they cannot be pleased or angered.

9

MANEUVERING ARMIES

This means choosing the most advantageous ways to go.

> Whenever you station an army to observe an opponent, cut off the mountains and stay by the valleys.

> Watch the light, stay on the heights. When fighting on a hill, do not climb. This applies to an army in the mountains.

One version says, "Fight going down, not climbing up."

> When cut off by water, always stay away from the water. Do not meet them in the water; it is advanta-

geous to let half of them cross and then attack them.

When you want to fight, do not face an enemy near water. Watch the light, stay in high places, do not face the current of the water. This applies to an army on water.

In a river basin your armies can be flooded out, and poison can be put in the streams. Facing the current means heading against the flow. It also means your boats should not be moored downstream, lest the enemy ride the current right over you.

Go right through salt marshes, just go quickly and do not tarry. If you run into an army in the middle of a salt marsh, stay by the water-plants, with your back to the trees. This applies to an army in a salt marsh.

On a level plateau, take up positions where it is easy to maneuver,

> **keeping higher land to your right rear, with low ground in front and high ground behind. This applies to an army on a plateau.**

> **It was by taking advantage of the situation in these four basic ways that the Yellow Emperor overcame four lords.**

All martial arts began with the Yellow Emperor [a Taoist ruler of late prehistoric times, ca. 2400 B.C.E.], so he is mentioned here.

> **Ordinarily, an army likes high places and dislikes low ground, values light and despises darkness.**

High places are exhilarating, so people are comfortable, and they are also convenient for the force of momentum. Low ground is damp, which promotes illnesses, and makes it hard to fight.

> **Take care of physical health and stay where there are plenty of re-**

sources. When there is no sickness in the army, it is said to be invincible.

Where there are hills or embankments keep on their sunny side, with them to your right rear. This is an advantage to a military force, the help of the land.

Advantage in a military operation is getting help from the land.

When it rains upstream and froth is coming down on the current, if you want to cross, wait until it settles.

Whenever the terrain has impassable ravines, natural enclosures, natural prisons, natural traps, natural pitfalls, and natural clefts, you should leave quickly and not get near them. For myself, I keep away from these, so that opponents are nearer to them; I keep

my face to these so that opponents
have their backs to them.

Then you have the advantage, and he is out
of luck.

When an army is traveling, if there
is hilly territory with many
streams and ponds or depressions
overgrown with reeds, or wild forests with a luxuriant growth of
plants and trees, it is imperative to
search them carefully and thoroughly. For these afford stations
for bushwhackers and spoilers.

It is imperative to dismount and search,
lest there be ambush troops hiding in such
places. Also, there is concern that spies
might be lurking there watching you and
listening to your directives.

When the enemy is near but still,
he is resting on a natural stronghold. When he is far away but tries
to provoke hostilities, he wants

**you to move forward. If his posi-
tion is accessible, it is because that
is advantageous to him.**

What this means is that if an opponent
does not keep a position on a natural
stronghold but stations himself in a convenient place, it must be because there is
some practical advantage in doing so.

**When the trees move, the enemy is
coming; when there are many
blinds in the undergrowth, it is
misdirection.**

The idea of making many blinds in the un-
derbrush is to make you think there might
be bushwhackers hidden behind them.

**If birds start up, there are am-
bushers there. If the animals are
frightened, there are attackers
there. If dust rises high and sharp,
vehicles are coming; if it is low and
wide, footsoldiers are coming.
Scattered wisps of smoke indicate**

woodcutters. Relatively small amounts of dust coming and going indicate setting up camp.

Those whose words are humble while they increase war preparations are going to advance. Those whose words are strong and who advance aggressively are going to retreat.

If his emissaries come with humble words, send spies to observe him and you will find that the enemy is increasing his preparations.

When light vehicles come out first and stay to the sides, they are going to set up a battle line.

Those who come seeking peace without a treaty are plotting.

Those who busily set out arrays of armed vehicles are expecting reinforcements.

They wouldn't rush around for an ordinary rendezvous—there must be a distant force expected at a certain time, when they will join forces to come and attack you. It is best to prepare for this right away.

If half their force advances and half retreats, they are trying to lure you.

They feign confusion and disorder to lure you into moving forward.

If they brace themselves as they stand, they are starving. When those sent to draw water first drink themselves, they are thirsty.

When they see an advantage but do not advance on it, they are weary.

If birds are gathered there, the place has been vacated.

If there are birds on a citadel, the army has fled.

If there are calls in the night, they are afraid.

They are fearful and uneasy, so they call to each other to strengthen themselves.

If the army is unsettled, it means the general is not taken seriously.

If signals move, that means they are in confusion.

Signals are used to unify the group, so if they move about unsteadily, it means the ranks are in disarray.

If their emissaries are irritable, it means they are tired.

When they kill their horses for meat, it means that the soldiers have no food; when they have no pots and do not go back to their quarters, they are desperate adversaries.

When there are murmurings, lapses in duties, and extended con-

versations, the loyalty of the group has been lost.

Murmurings describe talk of true feelings, lapses in duties indicate trouble with superiors. When the military leadership has lost the people's loyalty, they talk to each other frankly about the trouble with their superiors.

When they give out numerous rewards, it means they are at an impasse; when they give out numerous punishments, it means they are worn out.

When the force of their momentum is exhausted, they give repeated rewards to please their soldiers, lest they rebel en masse. When people are so worn out that they cannot carry out orders, they are punished again and again to establish authority.

To be violent at first and wind up fearing one's people is the epitome of ineptitude.

Those who come in a conciliatory manner want to rest.

When forces angrily confront you but delay engagement, yet do not leave, it is imperative to watch them carefully.

They are preparing a surprise attack.

In military matters it is not necessarily beneficial to have more strength, only to avoid acting aggressively; it is enough to consolidate your power, assess opponents, and get people, that is all.

The individualist without strategy who take opponents lightly will inevitably become the captive of others.

If you have no ulterior scheme and no forethought, but just rely on your individual bravery, flippantly taking opponents lightly and giving no consideration to the situation, you will surely be taken prisoner.

If soldiers are punished before a personal attachment to the leadership is formed, they will not submit, and if they do not submit they are hard to employ.

If punishments are not executed after personal attachment has been established with the soldiers, then they cannot be employed.

When there are underlying feelings of appreciation and trust, and the hearts of the soldiers are already bonded to the leadership, if punishments are relaxed the soldiers will become haughty and impossible to employ.

Therefore direct them through cultural arts, unify them through martial arts; this means certain victory.

Cultural art means humaneness, martial art means law. Command them humanely and benevolently, unify them strictly and sternly. When benevolence and sternness are both evident, it is possible to be sure of victory.

> When directives are consistently carried out to edify the populace, the populace accepts. When directives are not consistently carried out to edify the populace, the populace does not accept. When directives are consistently carried out, there is mutual satisfaction between the leadership and the group.

10
TERRAIN

Some terrain is easily passable, in some you get hung up, some makes for a standoff, some is narrow, some is steep, some is wide open.

When both sides can come and go, the terrain is said to be easily passable. When the terrain is easily passable, take up your position first, choosing the high and sunny side, convenient to supply routes, for advantage in battle.

When you can go but have a hard time getting back, you are said to be hung up. On this type of terrain, if the opponent is unprepared, you will prevail if you go forth, but if the enemy is prepared, if you go forth and do not prevail you will have a hard time getting back, to your disadvantage.

When it is disadvantageous for either side to go forth, it is called standoff terrain. On standoff terrain, even though the opponent offers you an advantage, you do not go for it—you withdraw, inducing the enemy half out, and then you attack, to your advantage.

On narrow terrain, if you are there first, you should fill it up to await the opponent. If the opponent is there first, do not pursue if the opponent fills the narrows. Pursue if the opponent does not fill the narrows.

On steep terrain, if you are there first, you should occupy the high and sunny side to await the opponent. If the opponent is there first, withdraw from there and do not pursue.

On wide-open terrain, the force of momentum is equalized, and it is hard to make a challenge, disadvantageous to fight.

Understanding these six kinds of terrain is the highest responsibility of the general, and it is imperative to examine them.

These are the configurations of terrain; generals who do not know them lose.

So among military forces there are those who rush, those who tarry, those who fall, those who crumble, those who riot, and those who get beaten. These are not natural disasters, but faults of the generals.

Those who have equal momentum but strike ten with one are in a rush. Those whose soldiers are strong but whose officers are weak tarry. Those whose officers are strong but whose soldiers are weak fall. When colonels are angry and obstreperous and fight on their own out of spite when they meet opponents, and the generals do not know their abilities, they crumble.

Generally speaking, the entire military leadership has to be of one mind, all of the military forces have to cooperate, in order to be able to defeat opponents.

When the generals are weak and lack authority, instructions are not clear, officers and soldiers lack consistency, and they form battle lines every which way, this is riot. When the generals cannot assess opponents, clash with much greater numbers or more powerful forces, and do not sort out the levels of skill among their own troops, these are the ones who get beaten.

If you employ soldiers without sorting out the skilled and unskilled, the brave and the timid, you are bringing defeat on yourself.

These six are ways to defeat. Understanding this is the ultimate responsibility of the generals; they must be examined.

First is not assessing numbers, second is lack of a clear system of punishments and rewards, third is failure in training, forth is irrational overexcitement, fifth is ineffectiveness of law and order, and sixth is failure to choose the strong and resolute.

The contour of the land is an aid to an army; sizing up opponents to determine victory, assessing dangers and distances, is the proper course of action for military leaders. Those who do battle knowing these will win, those who do battle without knowing these will lose.

Therefore, when the laws of war indicate certain victory it is surely appropriate to do battle, even if the government says there is to be no battle. If the laws of war do not

indicate victory, it is appropriate not to do battle, even if the government orders war. Thus one advances without seeking glory, retreats without avoiding blame, only protecting people, to the benefit of the government as well, thus rendering valuable service to the nation.

Advancing and retreating contrary to government orders is not done for personal interest, but only to safeguard the lives of the people and accord with the true benefit of the government. Such loyal employees are valuable to a nation.

Look upon your soldiers as you do infants, and they willingly go into deep valleys with you; look upon your soldiers as beloved children, and they willingly die with you.

If you are so nice to them that you cannot employ them, so kind to them that you cannot command

them, so casual with them that you cannot establish order, they are like spoiled children, useless.

Rewards should not be used alone, punishments should not be relied on in isolation. Otherwise, like spoiled children, people will become accustomed to either enjoying or resenting everything. This is harmful and renders them useless.

If you know your soldiers are capable of striking, but do not know whether the enemy is invulnerable to a strike, you have half a chance of winning. If you know the enemy is vulnerable to a strike, but do not know if your soldiers are incapable of making such a strike, you have half a chance of winning. If you know the enemy is vulnerable to a strike, and know your soldiers can make the strike, but do not know if the lay of the land makes it unsuitable for battle, you have half a chance of winning.

Therefore those who know martial arts do not wander when they move, and do not become exhausted when they rise up. So it is said that when you know yourself and others, victory is not in danger; when you know sky and earth, victory is inexhaustible.

11

NINE GROUNDS

According to the rule for military operations, there are nine kinds of ground. Where local interests fight among themselves on their own territory, this is called a ground of dissolution.

When the soldiers are attached to the land and are near home, they fall apart easily.

When you enter others' land, but not deeply, this is called light ground.

This means the soldiers can all get back easily.

Land that would be advantageous to you if you got it and to opponents if they got it is called ground of contention.

A ground of inevitable contention is any natural barricade or strategic pass.

Land where you and others can come and go is called a trafficked ground.

Land that is surrounded on three sides by competitors and would give the first to get it access to all the people on the continent is called intersecting ground.

Intersecting ground means the intersections of main arteries linking together numerous highway systems: first occupy this ground, and the people will have to go with you. So if you get it you are secure, if you lose it you are in peril.

When you enter deeply into others' land, past many cities and towns, this is called heavy ground.

This is ground from which it is hard to return.

When you traverse mountain forests, steep defiles, marshes, or any route difficult to travel, this is called bad ground.

When the way in is narrow and the way out is circuitous, so a small enemy force can strike you, even though your numbers are greater, this is called surrounded ground.

If you are capable of extraordinary adaptation, you can travel this ground.

When you will survive if you fight quickly and perish if you do not, this is called dying ground.

People on dying ground are, as it were, sitting in a leaking boat, lying in a burning house.

So let there be no battle on a ground of dissolution, let there be no stopping on light ground, let there be no attack on a ground of contention, let there be no cutting off of trafficked ground. On intersecting ground form communications, on heavy ground plunder, on bad ground keep going, on surrounded ground make plans, on dying ground fight.

On a ground of dissolution, the soldiers might run away. Light ground is where soldiers have first entered enemy territory and do not yet have their backs to the wall; hence the minds of the soldiers are not really concentrated, and they are not ready for battle. It is not advantageous to attack an enemy on a ground of contention; what is advantageous is to get there first. Trafficked ground should not be cut off, so that the roads may be used advantageously as supply routes. On intersecting ground, if you establish alliances you are safe, if you lose alliances you are in peril. On heavy ground, plundering means building up supplies. On bad ground, since you cannot entrench, you should make haste to

leave there. On surrounded ground, bring
surprise tactics into play. If they fall into
dying ground, then everyone in the army
will spontaneously fight. This is why it is
said, "Put them on dying ground, and then
they will live."

> Those who are called the good
> militarists of old could make op-
> ponents lose contact between
> front and back lines, lose reliabil-
> ity between large and small
> groups, lose mutual concern for
> the welfare of the different social
> classes among them, lose mutual
> accommodation between the ru-
> lers and the ruled, lose enlistments
> among the soldiers, lose coherence
> within the armies. They went into
> action when it was advantageous,
> stopped when it was not.

They set up changes to confuse their opponents, striking them here and there, ter-
rorizing and disarraying them in such a
way that they had no time to plan.

It may be asked, when a large, well-organized opponent is about to come to you, how do you deal with it? The answer is that you first take away what they like, and then they will listen to you.

The condition of a military force is that its essential factor is speed, taking advantage of others' failure to catch up, going by routes they do not expect, attacking where they are not on guard.

This means that to take advantage of unpreparedness, lack of foresight, or lack of caution on the part of opponents, it is necessary to proceed quickly, it won't work if you hesitate.

In general, the pattern of invasion is that invaders become more intense the farther they enter alien territory, to the point where the native rulership cannot overcome them.

Glean from rich fields, and the armies will have enough to eat. Take care of your health and avoid stress, consolidate your energy and build up your strength. Maneuver your troops and assess strategies so as to be unfathomable.

Consolidate your keenest energy, save up your extra strength, keep your form concealed and your plans secret, being unfathomable to enemies, waiting for a vulnerable gap to advance upon.

Put them in a spot where they have no place to go, and they will die before fleeing. If they are to die there, what can they not do? Warriors exert their full strength. When warriors are in great danger, then they have no fear. When there is nowhere to go they are firm, when they are deeply involved they stick to it. If they have no choice, they will fight.

For this reason the soldiers are alert without being drilled, enlist without being drafted, are friendly without treaties, are trustworthy without commands.

This means that when warriors are in mortal danger everyone high and low has the same aim, so they are spontaneously on the alert without being drilled, are spontaneously sympathetic without being drafted, and are spontaneously trustworthy without treaties or commands.

Prohibit omens to get rid of doubt, and soldiers will never leave you. If your soldiers have no extra goods, it is not that they dislike material goods. If they have no more life, it is not that they do not want to live long. On the day the order to march goes out, the soldiers weep.

So a skillful military operation should be like a swift snake that

counters with its tail when someone strikes at its head, counters
with its head when someone
strikes at its tail, and counters
with both head and tail when
someone strikes at its middle.

This represents the method of a battle line, responding swiftly when struck. A manual of eight classical battle formations says, "Make the back the front, make the front the back, with four heads and eight tails. Make the head anywhere, and when the enemy lunges into the middle, head and tail both come to the rescue."

The question may be asked, can a
military force be made to be like
this swift snake? The answer is
that it can. Even people who dislike each other, if in the same
boat, will help each other out in
trouble.

It is the force of the situation that makes this happen.

Therefore tethered horses and buried wheels are not sufficiently reliable.

Horses are tethered to make a stationary battle line, wheels are buried to make the vehicles immovable. Even so, this is not sufficiently secure and reliable. It is necessary to allow adaptation to changes, placing soldiers in deadly situations so that they will fight spontaneously, helping each other out like two hands—this is the way to security and certain victory.

To even out bravery and make it uniform is the Tao of organization. To be successful with both the hard and soft is based on the pattern of the ground.

If you get the advantage of the ground, you can overcome opponents even with soft, weak troops—how much the more with hard, strong troops? What makes it possible for both strong and weak to be useful is the configuration of the ground.

Therefore those skilled in military operations achieve cooperation in a group so that directing the group is like directing a single individual with no other choice.

The business of the general is quiet and secret, fair and orderly.

His plans are calm and deeply hidden, so no one can figure them out. His regime is fair and orderly, so no one dares take him lightly.

He can keep the soldiers unaware, make them ignorant.

He changes his actions and revises his plans, so that people will not recognize them. He changes his abode and goes by a circuitous route, so that people cannot anticipate him.

When people never understand what your intention is, then you win. The Great White Mountain Man said, "The reason deception is valued in military operations is not just for deceiving enemies, but to begin with for deceiving one's own troops, to get them to follow unknowingly."

> When a leader establishes a goal with the troops, he is like one who climbs up to a high place and then tosses away the ladder. When a leader enters deeply into enemy territory with the troops, he brings out their potential. He has them burn the boats and destroy the pots, drives them like sheep, none knowing where they are going.

> To assemble armies and put them into dangerous situations is the business of generals. Adaptations to different grounds, advantages of contraction and expansion, patterns of human feelings and conditions—these must be examined.

When he talks about the advantages and disadvantages of contraction and expansion, he means that the ordinary patterns of human feelings all change according to the various types of ground.

Generally, the way it is with invaders is that they unite when deep in enemy territory but are prone to dissolve while on the fringes. When you leave your country and cross the border on a military operation, that is isolated ground. When it is accessible from all directions, it is trafficked ground. When penetration is deep, that is heavy ground. When penetration is shallow, that is light ground. When your back is to an impassable fastness and before you are narrow straits, that is surrounded ground. When there is nowhere to go, that is deadly ground.

So on a ground of dissolution, I would unify the minds of the troops. On light ground, I would have them keep in touch. On a

ground of contention, I would
have them follow up quickly. On
an intersecting ground, I would be
careful about defense. On a trafficked ground, I would make alliances firm. On heavy ground, I
would ensure continuous supplies.
On bad ground, I would urge them
onward. On surrounded ground, I
would close up the gaps. On
deadly ground, I would indicate to
them there is no surviving.

So the psychology of soldiers is
to resist when surrounded, fight
when it cannot be avoided, and
obey in extremes.

Not until soldiers are surrounded do they
each have the determination to resist the
enemy and sustain victory. When they are
desperate, they put up a united defense.

Therefore those who do not know
the plans of competitors cannot
prepare alliances. Those who do

not know the lay of the land cannot maneuver their forces. Those who do not use local guides cannot take advantage of the ground. The military of an effective rulership must know all these things.

When the military of an effective rulership attacks a large country, the people cannot unite. When its power overwhelms opponents, alliances cannot come together.

If you are able to find out opponents' plans, take advantage of the ground, and maneuver opponents so that they are helpless, then even a large country cannot assemble enough people to stop you.

Therefore if you do not compete for alliances anywhere, do not foster authority anywhere, but just extend your personal influence, threatening opponents, this makes town and country vulnerable.

Give out rewards that are not in the rules, give out directives that are not in the code.

Consider the merit to give the reward, without rules set up beforehand; observe the opponent to make promises, without prior setup of codes.

Employ the entire armed forces like employing a single person. Employ them with actual tasks, do not talk to them. Motivate them with benefits, do not tell them about harm.

Just employ them to fight, don't tell them your strategy. Let them know what benefit there is in it for them, don't tell them about the potential harm. If the truth leaks out, your strategy will be foiled. If the soldiers worry, they will be hesitant and fearful.

Confront them with annihilation, and they will then survive; plunge

them into a deadly situation, and they will then live. When people fall into danger, they are then able to strive for victory.

So the task of a military operation is to accord deceptively with the intentions of the enemy. If you concentrate totally on the enemy, you can kill its military leadership a thousand miles away. This is skillful accomplishment of the task.

First you go along with their intentions, subsequently you kill their generals — this is skill in accomplishing the task.

So on the day war is declared, borders are closed, passports are torn up, and emissaries are not let through.

Matters are dealt with strictly at headquarters.

Strictness at headquarters in the planning stage refers to secrecy.

When opponents present openings, you should penetrate them immediately. Get to what they want first, subtly anticipate them. Maintain discipline and adapt to the enemy in order to determine the outcome of the war. Thus, at first you are like a maiden, so the enemy opens his door; then you are like a rabbit on the loose, so the enemy cannot keep you out.

12

FIRE ATTACK

There are five kinds of fire attack: burning people, burning supplies, burning equipment, burning storehouses, and burning weapons.

The use of fire must have a basis, and requires certain tools. There are appropriate times for setting fires, namely when the weather is dry and windy.

Generally, in fire attacks it is imperative to follow up on the crises caused by the fires. When fire is set inside an enemy camp, then respond quickly from outside. If the soldiers are calm when fire breaks out, wait—do not attack. When the fire reaches the height of its power, follow up if possible, hold back if not.

In general, fire is used to throw enemies into confusion so that you can attack them.

> When fire can be set out in the open, do not wait until it can be set inside a camp—set it when the time is right.

> When fire is set upwind, do not attack downwind.

It is not effective to go against the momentum of the fire, because the enemy will surely fight to the death.

> If it is windy during the day, the wind will stop at night.

A daytime wind will stop at night, a night wind will stop at daylight.

> Armies must know there are adaptations of the five kinds of fire attack, and adhere to them scientifically.

It will not do just to know how to attack others with fire, it is imperative to know how to prevent others from attacking you.

> So the use of fire to help an attack means clarity, use of water to help at attack means strength. Water can cut off, but cannot plunder.

Water can be used to divide up an opposing army, so that their force is divided and yours is strong.

> To win in battle or make a successful siege without rewarding the meritorious is unlucky and earns the name of stinginess. Therefore it is said that an enlightened government considers this, and good military leadership rewards merit. They do not mobilize when there is no advantage, do not act when there is nothing to gain, do not fight when there is no danger.

Armaments are instruments of ill omen, war is a dangerous affair. It is imperative to prevent disastrous defeat, so it will not do to mobilize an army for petty reasons—arms are only to be used when there is no choice but to do so.

A government should not mobilize an army out of anger, military leaders should not provoke war out of wrath. Act when it is beneficial, desist if it is not. Anger can revert to joy, wrath can revert to delight, but a nation destroyed cannot be restored to existence, and the dead cannot be restored to life. Therefore an enlightened government is careful about this, a good military leadership is alert to this. This is the way to secure a nation and keep the armed forces whole.

13

ON THE USE
OF SPIES

A major military operation is a severe drain on the nation, and may be kept up for years in the struggle for one day's victory. So to fail to know the conditions of opponents because of reluctance to give rewards for intelligence is extremely inhumane, uncharacteristic of a true military leader, uncharacteristic of an assistant of the government, uncharacteristic of a victorious chief. So what enables an intelligent government and a wise military leadership to overcome others and achieve extraordinary accomplishments is foreknowledge.

Foreknowledge cannot be gotten from ghosts and spirits, cannot be had by analogy, cannot be found out by calculation. It must be obtained from people, people who know the conditions of the enemy.

There are five kinds of spy: The local spy, the inside spy, the reverse spy, the dead spy, and the living spy. When the five kinds of spies are all active, no one knows their routes—this is called organizational genius, and is valuable to the leadership.

Local spies are hired from among the people of a locality. Inside spies are hired from among enemy officials. Reverse spies are hired from among enemy spies. Dead spies transmit false intelligence to enemy spies. Living spies come back to report.

Among officials of the opposing regime, there are those that can be secretly ap-

proached and bribed so as to find out conditions in their country and discover any
plans against you; they can also be used to
create rifts and disharmony.

> Therefore no one in the armed
> forces is treated as familiarly as are
> spies, no one is given rewards as
> rich as those given to spies, and no
> matter is more secret than espio-
> nage.

If spies are not treated well, they may become renegades and work for the enemy.

> One cannot use spies without sa-
> gacity and knowledge, one cannot
> use spies without humanity and
> justice, one cannot get the truth
> from spies without subtlety. This
> is a very delicate matter indeed.
> Spies are useful everywhere.

Every matter requires prior knowledge.

> If an item of intelligence is heard
> before a spy reports it, then both

the spy and the one who told about it die.

Whenever you want to attack an army, besiege a city, or kill a person, first you must know the identities of their defending generals, their associates, their visitors, their gatekeepers, and their chamberlains, so have your spies find out.

Whenever you are going to attack and fight, first you have to know the talents of the people employed by the opponent, so you can deal with them according to their abilities.

You must seek out enemy agents who have come to spy on you, bribe them and induce them to stay with you, so you can use them as reverse spies. By intelligence thus obtained, you can find local spies and inside spies to employ. By intelligence thus obtained, you can cause the misinformation of dead spies to be conveyed to the enemy. By intelligence thus obtained, you can get living spies to work as planned.

It is essential for a leader to know about the five kinds of espionage, and this knowledge depends on reverse spies, so reverse spies must be treated well.

So only a brilliant ruler or a wise general who can use the highly intelligent for espionage is sure of great success. This is essential for military operations, and the armies depend on this in their actions.

It will not do for the army to act without knowing the opponent's condition, and to know the opponent's condition is impossible without espionage.